San Francisco

The Alphabet Book

By: Matt Weber

www.121publications.com

B is for the **Bridges**

Bay Bridge and Golden Gate
Both of them were open
By nineteen thirty-eight

Did you know...

...that both bridges are suspension bridges, meaning that their roads are hanging from cables draped over the towers?

...that the Bay Bridge has two sections that connect to a tunnel through Yerba Buena Island?

...that "Golden Gate" is the name of the strait that connects San Francisco Bay and the Pacific Ocean?

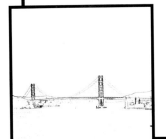

C is for a **Cable Car**

Clanging down the street
A more sure way to travel
Than slipping horses' feet

Did you know...

...that cable cars were started by Andrew Hallidie after he saw a horse-pulled trolley have an accident on a slippery hill?

...that the first cable car was operated on Clay Street in 1873 before automobiles were even invented?

...that in 1964 the cable cars were designated as a national historic landmark?

D is for **Dim Sum**

A tasty Chinese treat
When you visit Chinatown
There's lots of food to eat

Did you know...

...that Chinatown was first settled in the 1850's during the Gold Rush, and is the oldest Chinatown in the United States?

...that there are over 600,000 firecrackers used in the Chinese New Year parade each year?

...that "dim sum" means "touch the heart" in Cantonese?

E is **Embarcadero**

The street beside the bay
People jog past the piers
When it's a sunny day

Did you know...

...that "embarcadero" means "pier" in Spanish?

...that the Ferry Building, built in 1898, is located in the middle of the Embarcadero?

...that for over 40 years, the Embarcadero was a double-decker freeway until an earthquake in 1989 made it unsafe, which forced it to be removed?

F is for the **Fog**

Creeping from the seas
A cool white blanket sets
And brings a chilly breeze

Did you know...

...that it is rumored that Mark Twain once said, "The coldest winter I ever spent was a summer in San Francisco."?

...that fog is created when warm air moves over cold water, usually occurring in the summer in San Francisco?

...that one of San Francisco's nicknames is "Fog City"?

G is for the **Giants**

Let's turn some double plays
One of the very best
Was center-fielder Willie Mays

Did you know...

...that there are five San Francisco Giants in the Hall of Fame?
(Willie Mays 24, Orlando Cepeda 30, Willie McCovey 44, Gaylord Perry 36, and Juan Marichal 27)

...that the San Francisco Giants have played in three different stadiums? (Seals Stadium, Candlestick Park, and AT&T Park)

...that after the Giants moved from New York to San Francisco in 1957, they have been to the World Series three times? (1962, 1989, and 2002)

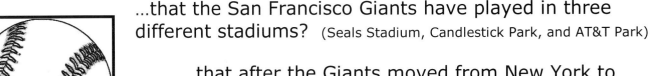

WILLIE MAYS
San Francisco Giants—Outfield

H is for the **Hills**

Atop the City sits
Nob Hill and Telegraph
A spot to look for ships

Did you know...

...that Coit Tower, on top of Telegraph Hill, was built in 1933 and is 210 feet tall?

...that Telegraph Hill was named after the nautical telegraph, a semaphore, that was located on top of it?

...that Telegraph Hill was once called Loma Alta (High Hill) by the Spanish and also was named Goat Hill?

I is for Angel **Island**

Across from Alcatraz
Coming to America
Immigrants did pass

Did you know...

...that between 1910 and 1940, 125,000 immigrants from Asia stopped at Angel Island before entering the United States?

...that in 1962 all of Angel Island became a state park?

...that Ayala Cove at Angel Island is named after Spanish explorer Juan de Ayala? (the first Spanish explorer to enter San Francisco Bay by ship)

J is for **Japantown,**

Chinatown, North Beach
Signs in other languages
You will find in each

Did you know...

...that Japantown is the oldest Japantown in the United States?

...that Russian Hill got its name because settlers during the Gold Rush discovered a Russian cemetery on the hill, from the days of the Russian otter hunters?

...that North Beach is also called "Little Italy" because many people of Italian heritage live there?

K is for the **Kites**
Flying in the air
Visit Crissy Field
You'll see a lot out there

Did you know...

...that Crissy Field is famous amongst kiteboarders, or kite-surfers, for its breathtaking views and high degree of difficulty?

...that each year the Family Day Kite Festival is held at the Marina Green, next to Crissy Field?

...that Crissy Field was an airport for the military and the post office between 1915 and 1974?

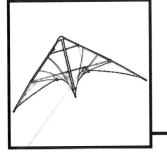

L is for sea **Lions**

That love to sit and bark
Walk along Pier 39
You'll see them until dark

Did you know...

...that San Francisco's largest group of sea lions once lived at Seal Rock, near Ocean Beach, but now they live at Pier 39?

...that the type of sea lion that lives near San Francisco is the California sea lion?

...that sea lions can get as heavy as 860 pounds and as long as eight feet?

M is for the **Mission**

Linking the City's past
Over two hundred years
Amazing it could last

Did you know...

...that Mission San Francisco de Asis was named after Saint Francis of Assisi?

...that the mission was founded on June 29th, 1776, which is even before the United States became a country?

...that the mission is also called "Mission Dolores", named after the nearby stream "Arroyo de Nuestra Senora de los Dolores", (*Stream of our Lady of Sorrows*)?

N is for the 'Niners

Our team is red and gold
The West Coast Offense
That won five Super Bowls

Did you know...

...that the 49ers have the nickname "Team of the 80's"?

...that the 49ers are named after the large number of people, called '49ers, who arrived in California in 1849 for the Gold Rush?

...that the 49ers have won five Super Bowls (1981, 1984, 1988, 1989, 1994) and have never lost a Super Bowl?

O is for the **Ocean**

Full of fish and whales
Large container ships
And little boats with sails

Did you know...

...that during some years, if enough sand gets moved by the waves, the top of a shipwreck is visible in the middle of Ocean Beach?

...that there used to be an amusement park at the beach, from 1926 to 1972, called Playland at the Beach?

...that Ocean Beach's most famous restaurant, the Cliff House, opened all the way back in 1863?

P is for the **Piers**

Where ferries come and go
Pier 39 is one
That many people know

Did you know...

...that Pier 39 has twelve restaurants, 110 shops, an aquarium, a carousel, and many performances?

...that there are even-numbered piers to the south of the Ferry Building and odd-numbered piers to the north of it?

...that there is a pier numbered 1½ from which the ferries to Sacramento previously departed?

Q is for the **Quakes**
More than just one time
1906 the City shook
And again in '89

Did you know...

...that the 1906 earthquake happened on April 18, at 5:12 AM and had a magnitude of 7.8?

...that the 1989 earthquake happened on October 17, at 5:04 PM and had a magnitude of 7.1?

...that the 1989 earthquake happened immediately before the third game of the World Series between the San Francisco Giants and the Oakland A's?

R is for the **Railroad**

Linking coast to coast
Four San Franciscans
Were to make the most

Did you know...

...that the transcontinental railroad was completed in 1869 and it connected San Francisco to the rest of the United States?

...that the "Big Four" were named Collis Huntington, Leland Stanford, Charles Crocker, and Mark Hopkins?

... there are hotels on Nob Hill named the Huntington Hotel, the Stanford Court, and the Mark Hopkins?

S is for **Sourdough**

A really tasty bread
Perfect for a chowder bowl
Or sandwiches instead

Did you know...

...that San Francisco's oldest sourdough bread company was started in 1849, during the beginning of the Gold Rush?

...that the bakers keep some dough, called the "mother dough", from each batch to be used in future baking?

...that San Francisco makes over 50 million loaves of sourdough bread each year?

T is **Transamerica**

The City's famous spire
At its very top
No other building's higher

Did you know...

...that the Transamerica Pyramid is the tallest building in San Francisco at 853 feet tall?

...that there are 3,678 windows on its 48 floors and it takes two months to wash them all?

...that the Transamerica building was built in 1972?

U is **Union Square**

Where cable cars will stop
You'll see lots of stores
Where people like to shop

Did you know...

...that Union Square was named because during the Civil War, people would gather there for rallies in support of the Union?

...that in the 1930's Union Square was the first place in the world that had an underground parking structure?

...that the four streets that border Union Square are Post, Geary, Stockton, and Powell?

V is for **Victorian**

They're everywhere you go
Fancy decorations
On houses in a row

Did you know...

...that the most famous Victorian houses in San Francisco are located on Steiner St. across from Alamo Square?

...that those houses are called "Postcard Row" and that Victorian houses are often nicknamed "Painted Ladies"?

...that over 48,000 Victorian houses were built in San Francisco between 1849 and 1915?

W is for the **Wharf**

Boats all bring their fish
Fishermen have for sale
Any seafood that you wish

Did you know...

...that Fisherman's Wharf gets over 12 million visitors a year?

...that two of the most popular foods at the Wharf are Dungeness crab and clam chowder in a bread bowl?

...that Domenico Ghirardelli came to California in 1849 during the Gold Rush and started his company in 1852? (now located next to Fisherman's Wharf)

X is for **Exposition**

A party from the past
San Francisco showed
That it was here to last

Did you know...

...that in 1915 San Francisco hosted the Panama Pacific International Exposition, to celebrate the opening of the Panama Canal?

...that the first transcontinental telephone line was built the same year, and during the Expo, people in New York listened to the Pacific Ocean over the telephone?

...that the Palace of Fine Arts was built for the Expo?

Y is **Yerba Buena**

The City's oldest name
A lot of mint was here
When Spanish people came

Did you know...

...that yerba buena (hierba buena) means "good herb (mint)" in Spanish?

...that the island connecting the two sections of the Bay Bridge is called Yerba Buena? (Treasure Island is next to it)

...that in 1847, the town of Yerba Buena officially changed its name to San Francisco?